Greening the
City Streets

Barbara A. Huff

Greening the City Streets

THE STORY OF COMMUNITY GARDENS

photographs by
Peter Ziebel

CLARION BOOKS

New York

Photo credits: page 33, The Library of the New York Botanical Garden, Bronx, New York; pages 28 & 35, New York City Parks Photo Archive; pages 31 & 32, Max Ulrich/New York City Parks Photo Archive.

Clarion Books
a Houghton Mifflin Company imprint
215 Park Avenue South, New York, NY 10003
Text copyright © 1990 by Barbara A. Huff
Photographs copyright © 1990 by Peter Ziebel

Huff, Barbara A.
    Greening the city streets : the story of community gardens / by
Barbara A. Huff ; color photographs by Peter Ziebel.
        p.   cm.
    Includes bibliographical references.
    Summary: A photo essay tracing the urban gardening movement in the
United States, with a special focus on the Sixth Street and Avenue B
Garden in Manhattan.
    ISBN 0-89919-741-8
    1. Community gardens—New York (N.Y.)—Juvenile literature.
2. Community gardens—United States—Juvenile literature.
3. Gardening—Juvenile literature.   [1. Community gardens—New York
(N.Y.) 2. Gardening.]   I. Title.
SB457.3.H84   1990
635′.09173′2—dc20   89-22193
                                                      CIP
                                                      AC

                    N W I   10 9 8 7 6 5 4 3 2 1

For Ann Brophy—
friend, writer, teacher, spur

Acknowledgments

My thanks and admiration go to all the members of the Sixth Street and Avenue B Garden, and to the people I talked to from other gardens across the United States and in London. Community gardeners are unfailingly enthusiastic, helpful, and committed.

Many other people generously shared their time and expertise. I am particularly grateful to Lisa Cashdan of the Trust for Public Land; Jane Weissman of Operation GreenThumb; Bea Orange of the Clinton Community Garden, and horticultural therapist Nancy K. Chambers at the Enid A. Haupt Glass Garden, Rusk Institute, and a big thank you to Peter Ziebel for taking all the terrific photographs.

Contents

Greening the
City Streets

Manhattan Island isn't just skyscrapers. At the feet of the tall buildings are more than one hundred thriving community gardens.

1

Greening the Mean Streets

In the springtime several years ago, gardeners were getting their land ready for planting. Long barren, the hard-packed ground needed deep cultivation to loosen and break up the soil. When the gardeners had dug down about ten feet, their shovels began to bring up bricks. Looking deep into the hole, they saw people far below them walking along a train platform. The gardeners had dug right through the brick roof of a subway station!

Finding a subway at the bottom of your garden isn't something that happens in farm country. The gardeners you will meet in this book don't live on farms in rural areas and measure their land in acres. They are community gardeners, usually families with children, and they live on a small island two miles wide by twelve miles long. The island is in the Hudson River off the coast of New Jersey. It's called Manhattan.

New York City is composed of five boroughs, each a separate county: Manhattan, the Bronx, Brooklyn,

Queens, and Staten Island. But to most people, New York City means Manhattan, site of the Empire State Building, Wall Street, Central Park, and the United Nations. One and a half million people live in Manhattan; hundreds of thousands commute to work there.

On that small, crowded island, there are over one hundred community gardens, and the other boroughs have several hundred more. In the last few years, these lush, productive gardens have grown up on vacant lots and other waste ground, usually in the poorest neighborhoods. Not all gardeners dig into the subway, but city gardening isn't like gardening anywhere else. It's full of surprises.

In an area half a mile square on Manhattan's Lower East Side, there are forty community gardens. They have names such as El Sol Brillante, the Miracle Garden, and the Green Oasis. One has a plain vanilla name. It's called the Sixth Street and Avenue B Garden, because that's where it is.

Let's visit Six and B and see what community gardening is all about.

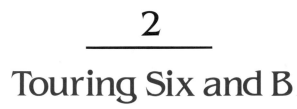

2

Touring Six and B

OUR TOUR STARTS on the sidewalk of Avenue B, a few steps from the corner of Sixth Street. Public School 64 is just behind us on the southeast corner. Right across the avenue from the school is the main gate, a wide opening in the high chain-link fence that encloses the garden. Most community gardens have fences to protect them and make them safe havens in sometimes rough neighborhoods. Garden members and garden friends all have keys, and when anyone is working or playing inside Six and B, the gate stands open in welcome.

Let's cross the street and stop just inside the garden. There's an open area here, stretching ahead to the apartment houses lining the garden on its far side. Straight across is a building the gardeners created that is part open-air stage, part meetinghouse, and part toolshed. Nearby are tables, benches, and a place for cookouts.

Just to our left are garden plots planted by kids from

Outside the fence are potholes and cracked sidewalks, but inside, flowers and vegetables flourish. The fireplug at right supplies the garden with water.

P. S. 64. There are also garden members' plots with vegetables and fruits and one whole plot full of sculptured toys, totem poles, and other figures.

Several paths branch out to the right. In midsummer it isn't easy to get through the garden because so much is growing. The plots seem to overlap in an abundance of green splashed with the red of tomatoes and apples, the gold of sunflowers and squash, and the purple of eggplant and onion flowers.

P.S. 64 can be seen through the fence. Behind the pre-kindergarten plot, another garden member has filled his space with toy sculptures and totem poles.

Future spaghetti sauce.

Find the bee. She's stocking up on nectar from the marigolds. Back at the hive, she'll help make honey.

Here and there are dwarf fruit trees—kid-accessible trees, one gardener calls them—that give plums, pears, and peaches to all the gardeners.

If we walk almost to Sixth Street and along to the far back corner of the garden, we'll come to the herb garden and a patch of lush grass. Like the fruit trees, the herbs belong to all the members. Taking another path, we'll soon come to apple trees and grape vines trained along trellises, which stand six feet high in midgarden.

Most of the gardeners' plots are four by eight feet, marked off with pieces of wood. The plots are only four feet wide so the gardeners can reach any area from the path. There's no need to step into a plot.

In a four-by-eight-foot plot like this one, a gardener grew forty-seven different kinds of plants.

Each of the nearly one hundred members, whether a single person or a family, has a plot. When it comes to making decisions affecting the garden, each member has one vote. And each member has a responsibility to the whole garden. To get a plot, you have to agree to go to monthly meetings and to give an hour a week of your time for whatever needs doing. Everyone pitches in to care for the herb garden, repair paths, or work on special projects such as repairing the stage.

What can you grow in a four-by-eight plot? Plenty! Here's a partial list of what the Six and B gardeners grow:

tomatoes · peppers · broccoli · cabbage · okra
collards · rhubarb · potatoes · horseradish
peas · string beans · broad beans · salad greens
herbs · leeks · onions · garlic
melons · grapes · squash · peaches
plums · pears · apples · cherries
strawberries · raspberries · blueberries
blackberries · gooseberries

Among the flowers that thrive at Six and B are chrysanthemums, columbine, roses, Johnny-jump-ups, pansies, petunias, hollyhocks, daisies, and snapdragons. In July the sunflowers reach skyward all over the garden. Sunflowers are immensely satisfying to grow because they shoot up almost before your eyes, and they tower dramatically over the garden. When the summer is over and the sunflowers die and dry out, the black-and-white seeds are simply delicious.

By summer, the plants escape their plot borders and take over the garden.

All of summer in one perfect bloom.

Many gardens have sunflower-growing contests with prizes for both the widest and the tallest.

Community gardens have many seasons. When one crop finishes its life cycle, plot gardeners dig up the old plants and replace them with a new crop. Each square foot of soil can produce several crops a year. Most of the gardeners use what is called the intensive method. That means using every inch of available space. The plants are grown so closely together that, by summer, hardly any soil shows between the green.

Our tour has brought us full circle and we're back at the P.S. 64 plots. You'll notice that the kindergarten plots are three feet wide instead of four feet. That's because young arms are shorter than fully grown ones and don't reach as far. These small plots are just the right size for young gardeners.

In community gardens, the members begin learning young. At Six and B, Garrick Beck, a garden member, holds thirty- to forty-minute morning classes each week during spring and summer. The classes give young kids hands-on gardening experience.

Garrick starts his garden classes with a tour like the one we've just taken. He explains some of the basic words used in gardening—soil, seeds, warmth, water, and sunlight. He points out that the plots are raised up a few inches above ground level for ease of use. Garden students learn to walk on the paths and not stomp around in the plots. Stepping in the plots may kill a plant. It also packs down the soil.

By the second week, the young gardeners are ready and eager to prepare the soil for planting. They turn over the earth and take out any weeds. They use hand

A Six and B member has his plot ready for planting.

Garrick Beck shows his garden class how to make a furrow using a basic garden tool, the trowel.

trowels for that kind of digging and also learn about other basic garden tools.

Garrick shows the kids how to make a furrow in the soil in which to plant a row of seeds. Radish seeds go in first. The next week they plant carrots, bush string beans, marigolds, and sunflowers. In only one week, the radishes have already poked their first leaves above ground.

When not working on their own plot, the kids tour the garden with Garrick and learn about the herbs and

Into the furrow goes the seed.

Watering plants can be hard, hot work, but it's necessary and worth the effort.

When your garden is four by eight feet, it's smart to help plants grow straight up.

some of the flowers. By late spring, green cherries and young peaches are already on the trees.

As spring turns into summer, Garrick's kids learn how to water their plot. Six and B is lucky. It usually doesn't have a problem getting water. The city allows the gardeners to take water from the corner fire hydrant. In addition to watering, children also learn how to pull up weeds without removing any of the other plants.

By the end of the month, the rest of the kids' plot is planted with tomatoes and pumpkins. The beans and carrots have come up, and the sunflowers are beginning to reach for the sky. Garrick shows the kids how to transplant cherry tomatoes and how to cultivate the soil by loosening it with trowel and fingers. The radishes are already big enough to pull up and eat.

By midsummer there's plenty to eat and plenty to do. The kids have beans, tomatoes, carrots, and radishes to take home for dinner. A bowl of garden marigolds or asters can be a dinner table centerpiece. The pumpkins, however, won't be ready until fall. When the last of the radishes and carrots have been eaten, the young gardeners plant broccoli and other late-summer and fall crops.

Other summer garden jobs include staking beans and tomatoes so that they grow up poles instead of sprawling along the ground and wasting valuable plot space. Community gardeners plant many crops that can grow vertically.

Also during the summer months, Garrick's kids learn to mulch around the base of the plants to hold in warmth and moisture. Mulch, which comes from a word

meaning soft or mild, is a protective covering. A layer of mulch protects the plants and also discourages weeds. Straw is Garrick's favorite mulch.

*

As we've wandered around Six and B, you may have noticed some of the wildlife in a city garden. On a summer day, the air is full of multicolored butterflies. Community gardeners welcome these bright scraps of color. They also encourage bees, which help pollinate the plants. Several gardens have beehives, and the members share the honey.

Dogs are usually banned in the official garden rules, although a well-behaved dog won't be thrown out. Two cats live at Six and B, but they work for a living. They help rid the garden of mice.

The gardeners of Six and B can plant anything they like in their own plots. One plot has had as many as forty-seven different kinds of plants. Some garden members grow only food, others grow mostly flowers. One member has a unique way of using his city garden plot. He fills it with grass, places a camp chair in the middle, and just sits there, enjoying life.

OPPOSITE: In summer the garden is a great place for playing.

Community gardens have something for everyone.

3

Gardens Aren't Just for Gardening

On THE GATE at Six and B, the members post a monthly schedule of garden events. As you read it, you quickly realize that a lot goes on in a community garden.

Kids' activities include T-shirt painting classes and other art projects. There are Garrick's classes for young gardeners, and the kids put on plays during the spring and summer months. Sometimes a troupe of visiting performers comes to Six and B, and the garden fills up with children watching jugglers and magicians. Also during the warm months, gardeners have picnics and cookouts.

A few of the hardier garden members sometimes get up at dawn to do a little bird-watching. New York City is on the Atlantic Flyway, a kind of sky-high freeway for migrating birds. Birds that fly south in the fall head north again in the spring, often making pit stops in city gardens. Early-rising bird-watchers can add rare birds to their sighting collections.

Community gardeners are considerate of their handicapped neighbors. Near the Six and B stage is a large, waist-high planting area just the right height for gardeners in wheelchairs. When a play is being performed, garden kids go to the nursing home a block away and help elderly people come to see the show.

"Gardening is good for you" could be the slogan of many elderly and handicapped gardeners. There's even a new branch of medicine that deals with the benefits of gardening. It's called horticultural therapy. Gardening is good exercise for people who need physical therapy, and it's much more fun than doing exercises over and over again. Retirees or people who can't find work feel better when they help their families by growing food.

Community gardeners see many examples of troubled young people who are helped by gardening. Growing things is a very positive activity. Plants respond to the care they're given by producing flowers and fruit and vegetables. Plants don't nag, the way a parent or a teacher may seem to do. A teenager in trouble works in a garden and achieves something meaningful.

Gardens aren't threatening. They are wonderful places for people who are old and unhappy, or young and unhappy. A plant doesn't care if someone is old or handicapped or in trouble. A plant repays everything, and more, that a caring gardener gives it.

Community gardens help their neighborhoods in still other ways. Six and B has a row of bins along the fence so that people can leave newspapers, cans, and bottles for recycling. Even the air quality seems better around the gardens. People who have allergic reactions to city dirt and pollution insist that the air is much fresher near gardens.

One of the most dramatic impacts community gardens have had is helping to lower the crime rate. Six and B blooms on land where crumbling tenements were once the headquarters for drug dealers and other criminals. With so many gardens in the area and so many neighbors spending time in them, the crime rate is way down.

Six and B got its start in the mid-1980s when the old tenement buildings that had been on that corner finally collapsed or burned down and the city cleared the rubble from the land. Neighbors in the area applied to a New York City agency called Operation GreenThumb for permission to lease the land and start a garden. OGT helped with the start-up money, as it has done for hundreds of gardens. The money paid for the fence and for tools and seeds. Then the gardeners were on their own.

Another Operation GreenThumb idea is Artists in the Garden, a program that commissions artists to paint murals on the walls bordering some of the gardens. Sculptors have also created art for gardens.

Six and B has been a community garden only since 1983, but already it has had a positive effect on the neighborhood. Like all the city's gardens, Six and B helps improve the quality of life, and as crime rates go down and residents take more pride in where they live, new people begin moving in and buying property.

The new families, many with young children, find they are in a part of the city facing both past and future. Helped by the community gardeners, the neighborhood

This garden with its painted mural looks like a quiet park, but there are vegetable plots just out of sight.

is on the way up. But old problems remain. In some parts of the city, the public playgrounds are still unfenced and open to drug dealers and other dangerous people. Parents who don't dare take their youngsters to such places often join a community garden. At first they may not be interested in gardening; they just want a safe place for their children to play. Later they may get involved in all sorts of activities and, eventually, sign up for garden plots. Community gardens like Six and B haven't been around for very long, but already a new generation is growing up in these green oases.

A community garden provides a safe and attractive place for a young family to relax.

The Children's Farm Garden in New York's Thomas Jefferson Park, 1910.

4

If It Grows Weeds, It Can Grow Vegetables

THE COMMUNITY GARDENS that are blooming all across the United States, and in many other parts of the world, are actually a new variation of an old idea. City people have created gardens before, but always as short-lived responses to emergencies. Wars and bad economic times have driven city dwellers to try growing their own food, but when the troubled years ended, their gardens were abandoned.

The first organized city gardening program was started by the mayor of Detroit. It all began in the early 1890s, when the country was in an economic depression. Many people were unemployed, and those who could find jobs worked for very low pay. The situation reached its peak in 1893, and that was when Mayor Hazen S. Pingree had his ground-breaking idea.

Mayor Pingree offered Detroit's poor the chance to grow some of their own food on city-owned vacant lots. People who were not earning money could still help provide food for their families, and with people growing their own food instead of buying it, the city saved money on welfare payments. Allotment gardening—gardening on plots allotted by the city—thrived.

Omaha, Baltimore, New York, Philadelphia, and Chicago were among the other cities that thought well of Mayor Pingree's plan and started their own vacant-lot gardening programs.

When the economy improved and people could again find work, they gave up their vacant-lot gardens. Then in 1914 came World War I, and with the war came food shortages. Everyone was encouraged by the government to plant a Liberty Garden. It was the patriotic thing to do. The U.S. School Garden Army was formed. Its purpose was to get children interested in growing food for their families and at the same time help the war effort. Like the gardens planted during the 1893 emergency, Liberty Gardens died away soon after the war ended in 1918.

The 1930s were another big time for urban gardening. During those dreadful years of the Great Depression, millions of out-of-work and desperately poor people gardened to survive. Helped by local and government advisors, they grew a limited range of basic foods—mostly potatoes and beans.

By the early 1940s, the world was at war again, and once more U.S. citizens were asked to help the war effort. The National Victory Garden Program was started to encourage people to plant gardens. Growing food at home helped in several ways: There would be more food available for the armed forces, the United States could

Highland Park Children's Garden, 1936. New York City helped children grow food for their families during the Great Depression.

send food to its allies in other countries, and food that was grown in Victory Gardens could be stored for the winter or for emergencies if the war got worse. Everyone, even the youngest child, could make a contribution to winning the war by caring for a Victory Garden.

Everyone gardened, in families and in larger groups. In 1944 40 percent of the food grown in the United States came from Victory Gardens. In 1945 the war ended, and fresh food from the country's farms was plentiful again. Food rationing ended, and the frozen food industry began to flourish.

Once more, urban gardening died away.

Park Farm Contest, 1939. These kids are proud to have grown such tall corn in the city.

During World War II, Americans grew almost half of their vegetables at home in Victory Gardens.

Today we're in the early years of the biggest urban gardening movement in history. There has never been anything like today's community gardens. Much has changed since the days of World War II, and the reasons city people garden have changed as well.

Two words were heard often in the late 1960s—ecology and environment. Informed and sensible people became concerned about the pollution of land, air, and water. More of us began to care about what we ate and how it was grown. At the same time, booming inflation caused food prices to soar. Another contribution to the rebirth of urban gardening was the fact that there were more people living in cities than ever before. Many of them came from overseas. They missed growing their own crops, and were glad to find garden space even in crowded cities.

Strange as it seems, cities had a surprising number of vacant lots. New York City is a good example of how that happened. It's hard to imagine open space in a small, crowded island such as Manhattan. But old buildings are often abandoned, especially in economic hard times, by owners who can't afford to keep them up. Then vandals move in and wreck the buildings or burn them down. Most of the empty lots that result are in poor neighborhoods—a small patch of ground here, another there.

New York City in the sixties was in the middle of an economic emergency. There was scarcely enough money

This converted vacant lot on Mulberry Street was one of the few parks available to New York City kids in the 1960s.

for basic services—schools, police, firefighters, road repair. Little money was left for nonessentials like taking care of parks, and none at all for building new recreational areas.

By the 1970s, the city had only 119 playgrounds for

two million children. That works out to fourteen thousand kids for every playground. To make it all worse, many playgrounds were overrun with drug dealers and addicts. New York City needed park space. City kids needed parks and safe places to play.

People in some of the worst neighborhoods began deluging the city with requests to use open spaces for gardens. The idea of gardens on public land wasn't completely new. The city's housing authority had started a garden program in housing projects a few years before.

In answer to the requests to use city-owned land, Operation GreenThumb was started in 1978. OGT operates out of the mayor's office and gets money from the federal government. It has helped more than six hundred garden groups get started. Block associations, church groups, schools, hospitals, day-care centers, drug rehabilitation centers, and senior citizens groups have all become involved in community gardens.

The city gardens of the past were used almost entirely for growing food. Today's gardens, and gardeners, are different. When Operation GreenThumb asked people why they become community gardeners, most of them said they wanted to improve their neighborhoods. The second most popular reason was the desire for really fresh food. After that came wanting more nutritious food. Gardening for fun came in ahead of saving money. Immigrants from Southeast Asia, Africa, and the Caribbean wanted to grow the types of food they knew in their old homes and couldn't find in the States. Many

One of the most important reasons for the success of community gardens has been the involvement of young people.

gardeners said they can or freeze food for the off-season.

Community gardeners share their harvest with shut-ins, the poor, and the elderly. No one knows better than a community gardener how much a garden improves the quality of life. All across the United States, community gardens are changing the way of life for city people. And wherever community gardens grow, across the country or around the block, young people are a vital part of their success.

The Green Oasis Gazebo.

5

It Isn't Easy Staying Green

THE EVIL MAGICIAN points his finger, and where a tree once grew, a concrete pillar now stands. He points again. Another tree disappears. Onto the scene roars a dragon. It chases the magician, weaving in and around the concrete pillars and remaining trees. The magician points his finger at the dragon. The dragon laughs. The villian tries other spells. Nothing works. The dragon closes in.

Then, to a big round of applause, the dragon gobbles up the evil magician and the play is over.

That's a rough description of a play put on by young people who are part of the Green Oasis Garden, a few minutes walk from Six and B. The magician represented land developers—a big threat to community gardens. The dragon, constructed by the kids, was fabulous. Its head was big enough for one actor to stand up in. The tail curved and wriggled through the garden, operated by hidden kid power. The play was such a success that the young actors are considering taking it on the road—to day-care centers.

Part of the Green Oasis kids' play took place in a handsome gazebo in the center of the garden's lawn. A gazebo is a freestanding building with a roof and open sides. The Green Oasis gardeners got the money for their gazebo as a result of a threat to the garden, not from developers, but from a movie company.

Spielberg Productions, a company headed by Steven Spielberg, wanted to film *batteries not included* on New York's Lower East Side in 1987. The company built its main set on a piece of waste ground on East Eighth Street, right across from the Green Oasis. The set designers created a tacky tenement building that was to be burned down at the end of the movie. The director wanted to show a really run-down neighborhood, but across from the set was the beautiful Green Oasis Garden.

Spielberg's production people got permission from the gardeners to cover their chain-link fence with plywood, blocking the garden out of all the movie shots. They promised to pay the gardeners for any damage. No one realized that during the months of shooting plants in the shadow of the fence would die from lack of sun.

The movie people became interested in the garden doings and were so sorry about the damage they'd done that they gave Green Oasis thousands of dollars. The money was used to replace the plants that had died, for spring bulbs and insurance, and to pay for the material out of which the gardeners built their gazebo.

The movie money will help with another plan as well. Dozens of kids from buildings on the block and from a nearby housing project hope to build a real stage on a strip of land next to the garden. They want to write, produce, and perform in bigger and better theatrical events. The Green Oasis kids are also planning to create a section with raised planting areas for people in wheelchairs.

Not many gardens are threatened by movie companies, but it's no coincidence that the Green Oasis evil magician represented developers. In New York and other cities across the country, land developers compete with community gardeners for valuable open city space.

Even though city officials may know how popular community gardens are, they are concerned that the land isn't bringing in revenue. After all, the gardens lease their land from the city for next to nothing. If a developer buys or leases city-owned land and puts up apartments or an office building, the city makes money from the sale or lease and is paid property taxes afterward. Many city officials see no tangible gains from community gardens. In New York and other cities, gardeners are constantly fighting to keep the bulldozers away from their gates. Kids are often an important part of the fight.

The Green Oasis play was an entertaining way to make people aware of the danger. Many people feel that the more visible community gardens are, the more their members talk up all the positive aspects, the less developers will want to seem like evil magicians bent on destruction.

Clinton Community Garden is part of the reason why this section of New York isn't called "Hell's Kitchen" anymore.

Over on the West Side of Manhattan, kids had a lot to do with raising the money that saved the Clinton Community Garden. In the early 1980s, the city was busy redeveloping an area that had once been called "Hell's Kitchen." Property values soared as new buildings went up and old buildings were repaired.

The city decided to take back the land it had leased to the Clinton Community gardeners and put it up for auction. Over the next few years, the city found it had a fight on its hands. The gardeners wrote letters and flooded the mayor's office with petitions. They were supported by such national organizations as the Trust for Public Land. More help came from a local volunteer group called the Green Guerillas, the very people who had dug into the subway when starting their own garden back in the seventies.

What turned the tide was the idea of Clinton member Bea Orange. "Let's sell the garden by the square inch," Bea suggested, "and buy it for the community." Of course, since the gardeners were only renting the land, they couldn't really sell it. They could ask for tax deductible contributions, though, and use the money to buy the garden from New York City. People who donated money to this good cause were given a pretend deed to a square inch of New York City.

One-third of an acre—the size of Clinton Community Garden—contains 2,160,000 square inches. One square inch sold for five dollars, a square foot for five hundred, and a square yard for five thousand. The buy-an-inch-of-New-York campaign eventually raised one hundred thousand dollars.

The families of Clinton Community launched a national advertising campaign, and sold buttons, T-shirts, and postcards. They even sold square-inch-campaign gift certificates.

The city had received a clear signal from thousands of people, many of them voters. One month before the auction, the city took steps that eventually resulted in the garden being leased to its members for continued open-space activity.

Everyone benefited. More than one hundred families

use Clinton Community for growing food and as their own park. The city found itself, almost accidentally, providing badly needed open space at no cost. It's not cheap to create and keep up park space in a crowded city. Community gardens cost the city nothing.

Happily, more and more officials are learning that community gardens give far more to the city than they cost it in lost taxes. Threats to the gardens remain, however. Many are bulldozed every year. But the gardeners have learned to fight back and to show how vital community gardens are to the quality of city life.

Kids growing up in the city's green spaces know it isn't easy staying green. But they are also learning that city gardeners are a strong and hardy species, tough as the city trees that spring up through broken cement. They don't give up easily.

OPPOSITE: Clinton Community Garden has a parklike lawn and many garden plots. The members also keep bees for their honey.

*The hardest job at the City Gardeners' Harvest Fair
must be deciding which vegetables get a blue ribbon.*

6

Harvesting All Year Long

At SIX AND B, another lush and fruitful summer is over. School has started, and in the circle of seasons, fall, the time of harvest, has arrived.

The pace of the garden slows down in the fall. Back in high summer, gardeners could hardly keep up with the fast-growing plants. Garden members practically lived outside—picking, eating, weeding, having cookouts, trying to stay ahead of the vegetables.

A highlight of late summer is the annual City Gardeners' Harvest Fair, held over an August weekend in Brooklyn. Any city resident can enter vegetables, flowers, plants, food, and crafts, and hope to win a blue ribbon. Entries from young people are judged separately. Vegetable classes include beets, cucumbers, sunflowers, and a category called "bountiful basket," which requires at least five different vegetables.

Exhibitors can enter their best marigold blooms or a garden bouquet, and there's a prize for the best container-grown tomato plant. For the cooking contest, categories include "creative coleslaw," "dietary guidelines cookies," fruit pies, and "edible horticulture art"—artistic arrangements of vegetables or fruit.

The harvest fair isn't just competition. 4-H clubs show farm animals; there are gardening workshops and environmental exhibits; the entertainment includes a bluegrass band contest, a children's clown show, country dancing, games, races, and plenty to eat.

Now that the main growing season is over, Garrick Beck's young gardeners can put into practice what they learned in the closing weeks of their gardening project. Garrick had taught the young gardeners how to plant a cover crop to protect and nourish the soil during the cold season. Six and B gardeners use alfalfa, clover, or wheat. Such crops can survive the bitter cold—overwintering, it's called.

Before the ground gets too cold to dig, many gardeners plant bulbs that will produce masses of flowers in the spring. Tulip, crocus, and daffodil bulbs need months of cold before they are ready to flower, so gardeners put them in the ground in late fall.

Even winter doesn't stop the gardeners of Six and B from enjoying their harvested crops. Garden members feast on spaghetti topped with sauce made from tomatoes, onions, and basil they have picked, cooked, and put into the freezer back in high summer. One gardener preserves seventy-three jars of stewed tomatoes, others freeze quarts of surplus snap beans. Another picks the mint that grows like a weed and turns it into mint tea. It

Winning a prize is great, but just being at the Harvest Fair is a high point of every summer.

keeps in her refrigerator for months. Each glass tastes like a summer day.

Just because the open ground is frozen and snow is on the way doesn't mean activity stops at Six and B. Many of the gardeners turn their plots into minigreenhouses. They build wooden frames over their gardens to a height of four or five feet. Heavy plastic covers the top and sides and is staked to the ground all around except for one section that opens so the gardener can reach inside.

Even a weak winter sun shining through the proctective plastic sheeting is strong enough to grow salad greens, collards, and herbs right through the cold months.

After Christmas the New York City Department of Sanitation collects cast-off Christmas trees and hauls them to a plant near the Hudson River. There the brittle, browning Christmas trees are shoved in one end of a huge mulching machine. The motor gnashes its metal teeth, and in a few seconds, out the other end of the mulcher shoot piney-smelling wood chips. One big tree makes about two shopping bags' worth of mulch.

The Green Guerillas collect truckloads of Christmas tree mulch to share among community gardens. At Six and B, some members spread mulch on their plots instead of planting a cover crop. Heaped around the base of fruit trees and where bulbs are planted, mulch acts like a blanket during the coldest days. Rain and melting snow running through the wood chips into the soil add nutrients.

Hidden under plastic covers, plants grow through the coldest months.

Spring comes to the garden. The flowers are back, and so are the bees.

After the Christmas trees have been harvested from the Sanitation Department and given new life as mulch, deep winter holds the garden. In February and March, the harvest is snow.

Waiting for the spring, community garden families plan for the new season, poring over seed catalogues. They discuss what worked well last year and what changes they might make: Beefsteak tomatoes instead of medium size? Sugar snap peas? Perhaps a row of marigolds; they help keep bugs away. How about more strawberries this year?

If there are a few warm days in February, a sharp-eyed gardener will spot the spiky leaves and perhaps even a flower climbing up from a crocus bulb planted in the fall. As March moves toward early spring, first the daffodils appear and then the tulips.

The first spring flowers are a sure sign that the ground is warming, the winter is over, and a new, productive year of gardening is about to begin.

Bibliography

Brooklyn Botanic Garden. *Community Gardening, A Handbook*. New York: Brooklyn Botanic Garden, 1979.

Fox, Tom, Ian Koeppel, and Susan Kellam. *Struggle for Space: The Greening of New York City 1970-1984*. New York: Neighborhood Open Space Coalition, 1985.

Ocone, Lynn and Eve Pranis. *The Youth Gardening Book*. Burlington, Vermont: National Gardening Association, 1983.

Numerous journals, newsletters, and other publications of the American Community Gardening Association; the National Gardening Association, New York City Council on the Environment; the American Horticultural Therapy Association; The Trust for Public Land; The Green Guerillas, and New York City Department of General Services' Operation GreenThumb; as well as publications of community garden groups across the United States and The National Federation of City Farms, Ltd., in Great Britain. *The New York Times* and other periodicals.

Gardening Organizations

For help and advice about community gardens in your area, contact:

American Community Gardening Association
The Pennsylvania Horticultural Society
325 Walnut Street
Philadelphia, PA 19106

Cooperative Extension Service
Listed in phone books under Cooperative Extension or the name of your county.

National Gardening Association
180 Flynn Ave., Burlington, VT 05401

American Horticultural Therapy Association
9220 Wightman Rd. Suite 300
Gaithersburg, MD 20879

The Trust for Public Land—National Headquarters
The Rialto Building, 116 New Montgomery St.
San Francisco, CA 94105-3607

Index

Page numbers in *italics* refer to illustrations.

635.0917 Huff, Barbara A.
HUF
         Greening the city
         streets.

$15.95   11754

© THE BAKER & TAYLOR CO.